5 Tiny Twists

Bringing dignity and respect back to the workplace

Gap Training Solutions

BethAnn Hengen Neynaber

© 5 Tiny Twists October 2014

elizabethneynaber@yahoo.com

www.gaptrainingsolutions.com

Prelude

A kaleidoscope is based on a mechanical principle of a tiny twist to the right or left and you have a new, intricate, stunning view of the particles of glass which make up the puzzle. The same principle will be applied to the principles of language in this book. The particles of glass are your clients and employees. They are strong and bright. They have the potential to fall together into the puzzle you desire to accomplish your goals when your language reflects the dignity and respect your team deserves.

Tiny twists can make a very large difference in the motivation, inspiration, creativity, endurance, loyalty and innovation of the people you serve. Yes – your role in leadership, customer service or sales comes with responsibilities. Many people are losing sight of the fundamentals of communication with dignity and respect which build their attributes in their teams and in their customer base.

A prime example: You would never begin a phone conversation or walk up to a person without beginning with a hello. Instant Message (IM) and text has become demanding, harsh and often without the human dignities of manners. The pace of business is used as an excuse.

The truth? Human beings always preform at top potential when dignity and respect are part of the formula of communication.

In every interaction you have the unique privilege of creating a positive twist or a negative, especially when you are in critical and visible positions with your clients and employees. Few interactions are neutral. Yes – it is time to step up to the responsibility of the position you have chosen and one you likely pursued with hard work, education and sacrifice.

Many people are baffled when two people apply for a position with the same education, comparative experience and a solid history of accomplishments and they are the one who does not receive the promotion. I am no longer surprised when I ask a sales person who does not make a major sale why they believe they didn't secure the sale and they answer with an honest, "I don't know, in fact some of our benefits were better and our price was in the ballpark."

Client service specialists will look outside themselves and blame the range of products they have or the promises of the sales person as the reason the client went to another firm.

In 20 years of National Sales, International Training, and Private Coaching I have heard the heartbeat of the employees in over 500 organizations and non-profit organizations. I have learned from employees who are motivated and inspired to excel by their bosses and company practices. I have learned the most from the ridiculously high numbers of employees who are striving to do their jobs with excellence and their supervisors or Senior Management teams who do not approach the privilege of leadership and customer interaction with the serious responsibility they carry in setting the momentum of success for the company.

The great news – you are here, having chosen this book to move to the next level of responsibility you have been charged by your role and privilege of supervising employees, securing clients or helping a company retain the customers they work so hard to secure. Get ready to gain practical, immediately applicable ways to take your language patterns to the next level to contribute to obtaining the goals and dreams you bring to the table.

Once you become aware of a pattern you need to change you have no excuse. If you ignore your gut instinct for a tiny twist you need to make you will be holding onto your own roadblock to success. This book is a bulldozer to the roadblocks of your success when you implement them!

Twist One: Stop Creating Your Own Stories

The cry to stop creating your own stories has come from so many different decision makers when interviewing companies as to why business was lost, and from so many employees nationally and internationally who are discouraged and not working at their potential, the list is so long it would fill an entire book.

Assumptive conversations do not treat the client or an employee with dignity or respect. The syndrome seems to ease into the patterns of the individuals with the most experience when they cease to follow the simple rule of remaining curious and take one experience and dump it into the conversation of another experience – especially when it smells like garbage.

A major health insurance company based in the Midwest moved a Vice President into the role of supervising a team whose clients were the sales and customer service teams of the organization. She began her role by walking into team members' offices and dumping her assumptive thoughts.

A highly motivated, talented, and high preforming team became confused, frazzled and filled with emotionally charged communication by a series of just four conversations – one for each office or cubicle she stopped in to meet the employee.

The manager was attempting to change the direction of the team and took no time to discover how they made decisions for the roles they played, what the clients said about their performance and services or where each team member's strengths laid. She refused to review resumes and accomplishments and even hired a contractor who was not competent in the expertise she sought although a team member had years of success in the tasks and would have completed the project while unifying the team. You guessed it – team members froze in their productivity, began to leave the organization and eventually the team was so dismantled a severance package was a welcome relief to the final walking wounded. Team members were so disillusioned by the experience they chose not to pursue other positions in the organization – losing years of investment by the organization in knowledge and award winning performers.

Assumptive conversations create a story, often without the actual facts, and lack all aspects of dignity and respect.

Salespeople and client service individual's worst habit is to tell the customer what the features and benefits of their company is - assuming the company's story is the client's story – and not asking the client what their story is! What benefits are important to them, what price point they are expecting, what is defined as excellence in customer service to them. Many younger workforce members believe IM and email is the key to relationships and many older workforce members refuse to embrace some of the technology preferences of the their client base. When asked recently in a sales training call if it was okay response to text a business owner with an answer my response was, "What does the client prefer?" I was not about to make up the story of what the client preferred.

The first step to stop creating stories is repeating this phrase before communication, "I am sure the individuals involved had solid reasons for the decisions they made and the actions they took and I need to learn the complete facts behind the challenge."

Open-ended questions are the twist to dignity and respect.

Asking a minimum of 3-5 open-ended questions before making decisions will provide you the critical information from the proper source – the individuals involved, not the story you could create from what you "think" happened or will meet the client's needs.

Whether it's an internal decision or a client based decision, the following open-ended questions will stop the pattern of creating your own story and allow you to gain a reputation for engaging employees and clients in the solutions needed.

- What are your expectations?
- What is your preferred method of communication?
- What is the timeline you are seeking?
- What would the ideal solution look like to you?
- Share with me what factors the client shared with you...
- How did you go about implementing the change?
- How has change like this been implemented successfully in the past?
- Who else needs to be involved in the decision?
- What has the client asked from you?
- Who was involved in the decision making process?

- What policies or guidelines did you use in the decision making process?
- What do you see as the strengths of your decision?
- What risks did you consider?
- How do you determine your priority projects?
- What data have you gathered and how have you applied it to this change?
- What expectations do you have for support?
- What are the resources you called on to assist you?
- What sphere of influence did you see being impacted by the process change?
- What were the phases of your original time frame?
- How did the original plans become altered?
- What contingence plans were developed?
- Where do you think the plans or implementation became derailed?
- What benefits were the goal of the change?
- Who else do I need to discuss the challenge with to understand all the details involved?
- How empowered were you to make the decisions you needed for success?
- When do you need the action to occur to satisfy the client?

Eliminate why questions from your choices. Why questions are a language choice which often creates a defensive posture for the individual.

- Please share with me how...
- What factors were involved when...
- Fill me in on how the decision was made to...

All of these phrases treat people with dignity and respect and allow the individual to tell you the really story.

Twist your perspective to curiosity and stop creating your own stories.

Twist Two: Begin with Acknowledgement

Let's review all the people who you interact with on a daily basis. Colleagues in the same position, the individuals who may report to you, the clients you serve (even in an operations position where your clients are internal team members) and all the support positions who handle the processes of the business: Your expenses, account payables, create the marketing material, training on new policies and procedures, and those who handle your technology needs for both you and the clients.

An average day may include 10 to 50, sometimes even 100 different individuals who provide you information, who interact with you for their services and product fulfilment or run the processes which keep the customers buying.

Each of these people have a role to play in your life and they assist you with your goals or dreams or host the power to derail you. Did you rebuff this bold statement? Take a minute and think it through. With each of these individuals you have an opportunity to create a reputation of credibility and integrity, the reputation of treating them with dignity and respect, and the opportunity to have fluid, mutually satisfactory communication with on a daily basis.

I want to be acknowledged for my contribution and capabilities before you ask me for more, more, more or significant change.

This cry is from the heart beat of your employees and clients.

What does this sound like?

Leadership Twist: "As we begin to review the process changes still needed, I want to thank you for the hours you have invested in this change and the priority you have created in your work flow for this project."

Excellence in Sales Twist: "As we review the timeliness of our delivery with you and your future product needs, I want to thank and acknowledge the individuals who have complied the concerns we are going to address and I want to thank you for your time and attention on how we can serve you with excellence."

Stellar Customer Service Twist: "As we review your monthly reporting I want to thank you for your time and for making this call a priority. Your attendance and input in this meeting is critical to us assisting you in accomplishing your goals and we will honor your input by completing a summary of our call today for your review."

Coaching for Confidence Twist: "As we review the aggressive goals for next year, your proven track record and dedication to serving clients with excellence are going to be the keys to our success with these goals and I am confident you have the skills and talents to meet or exceed these goals.

The responsibility of a position of visibility or leadership is to get outside yourself and to walk in the mind sets and heartbeats of the people in the meeting. When you meet someone where they are at they are much more likely to walk with you on the journey of the goals you need accomplished than if you expect them to always run to you and where your perspective lies.

The twist of acknowledgement is a mindset change for many. It is a conscious effort to treat colleagues and clients with dignity and respect for what is accomplished behind the scenes and many would say is simply "expected" for the employee to keep their job or the client to receive their products or services. You can dig your heels in and simply have expectations without acknowledgement and it is a guaranteed you will experience higher turner over, diminished client loyalty and lower productivity.

Acknowledgment is the responsibility of any client facing position and leadership role. Embrace this twist, begin to practice it today and experience the results of a more engaged workforce and a higher satisfaction rate for clients.

Twist Three: Encouragement is Always Successful

It would be difficult to believe there is a person reading this book who has accomplished something which took courage and confidence without the slightest bit of encouragement. Whether it was a teacher in your early years, a close friend , a spouse, or a family member, the individuals who have made history and brought the greatest innovations to the world have shared sometimes it only took one person believing in their ability or encouraging their dream.

The sad part? When I ask team members who the most influential or encouraging people are in their lives they rarely state a member of leadership in their organization. Occasionally team members will share one person in the company who inspires them and it is rarely their direct supervisor. When I ask how the individuals inspire them, the report is always the same: They encourage us to use our talents and introduce change by recalling for us the success we have already accomplished and how we can use that success to pave the way in the change.

I have experienced the privilege of reporting to some of the unique individuals who recognize how powerful simple encouragement can be and, in sales positions, I have watched these individuals work this magic with clients to secure business no one ever thought was possible.

Right now I have an email from a previous supervisor of mine which inspires me on a daily basis. It simply reminds me of some of my talent and encourages me to use it. This email encouraged me to go forward with this new series of books without her knowledge of how it would impact my courage to accomplish my goals.

I am also sorry to report I am just like my client base, I have also worked for some of the most self-focused bosses in the market place or engaged in discussions to provide them services. The positive of these experiences is I learned who I did not want to be as a supervisor.

Encouragement takes so little time – it does take a mindset twist.

The twist of encouragement requires a fundamental trust and belief that individuals have untapped potential and clients want to be part of their solutions. Inspiring courage will bring unprecedented results.

How do you begin to implement the twist of encouragement?

Step out of your life and your experiences and into the ideas of the other individual. When a sales person tells you they wish to exceed their goals and go on the national awards trip, immediately express your support they can accomplish anything they set their mind on.

When a client suggests they have some ideas on how to improve reporting, begin with how important it is for you to hear their ideas and how much you appreciate them providing you the opportunity to specifically address their ideas.

When a colleague is thinking about applying for a new job, stop with your concern about how it will impact the department and express how they have skills and talents in many areas and you would like to hear why the new job appears to be a fit for their talents.

Encouragement is all about others and nothing about the impact of change to you.

Yes, in a leadership role you want to bring discernment into the decision making process of what an employee might be suggesting and you can change your language to have the discernment provided in an encouraging way.

Bringing the twist of acknowledgment is how to start an encouraging conversation:

- I am sure you have solid reasons and experience to come forward with this idea and I welcome the chance to understand your thought process.
- I appreciate your constant engagement in improving the client experience and I am excited to hear your thoughts behind your suggestion.
- I thank you for being willing to take on the hard issues and I know you have the depth of experience to begin to determine new solutions for the team, let's set aside a time to really review your ideas.

When you host the discovery process meeting it too can be a time of showing respect and dignity to the time and courage the individual invested in presenting the new idea, innovation to a process or an elimination of a task or procedure.

- What challenges do you think this process will solve?
- What brought this challenge and need for change to your attention?
- What resources do you think will be needed to have it implemented?
- What do you believe the ROI will be and when will it be obtained?
- What do you think will happen if we don't consider the idea?
- What are the key benefits you see to the team and the company?

If time does not allow you to discuss the idea at the moment it is presented it is critical to acknowledge the individual's courage to present the idea and set aside a time to discuss the idea. It is appalling to me the number of times a team member has shared he/she saw a "train wreck coming" with a client or process, took a moment to let the manager know a challenge was forming and have an idea on how to address it and the manager has ignored or dismissed the concern.

What a missed opportunity to encourage and engage the entire team. You know that one team member can have huge influence in motivation and productivity of an entire team. The more solid the relationship is with the team the more influence the team member has. You can bet the team member has discussed the challenge with colleagues before coming forward. The team member may have the professional brand of "not throwing the manager under the bus" yet the team will notice how the manager responded. The grapevine is a company's strongest asset to success or the hidden reason productivity is not maximized.

The twist of encouragement will serve you well in all aspects of your life. As you begin to implement this twist in your professional life, you will be led to bring them into your personal life. If your response is – "But I do this with my children" – my thought would be: Then this will be very easy for you to immediately bring into your professional role.

Twist Four: Old fashioned manners are never overrated

As I sat in in the CEO's office of a very successful business in Tucson, AZ, I noticed 3 greeting cards plastered to the wall behind his door. I would not have noticed them except the meeting required the door be left open due to the number of individuals in the office and normally they are viewable only from his chair.

My initial thought was: If old fashioned manners were common, the man's wall would be filled with thank you cards for his contributions to the community and the people he has assisted in finding careers.

This artificially intimate age has evolved into abbreviations, excessive and spontaneous emotions being published to the world and communication one would never dream of saying to someone in person. Technology has created a window to the world concerning information and education and it has also diminished the dignity and respect in which individuals communicate with clients, colleagues and the people they supervise.

Just because you have access to Senior Management in your organization or at your client, does not mean you use the privilege.

There is an entire market for coaching because too many employees' careers have been derailed by emotional, disrespectful emails or bringing inappropriate people into a conversation because of failure to embrace professional protocol.

The CC of email is not your friend. Respect would be the process of working through your challenges with an individual directly, privately or with the intervention of an appropriate mediator. Many team members believe they can find support for a disagreement by copying individuals in different departments, the boss without a colleague's knowledge or the boss's boss inappropriately.

The embracing of formality in your communication and language can do nothing but serve you well. Many team members lament, "I can't believe they didn't talk to me first before exposing the issue to the world." Dignity means having the courage to keep disagreements as private as possible and notifying an individual if you feel the need to bring Senior Management into the discussion due to an inability to find a compromise. Occasionally it will serve you well to simply yield to the experience of the other individual and agree to disagree, no longer pursuing your opinion. Time often reveals the situation was not as critical as you believed at the time and you will be relieved you did not draw a line in the sand and pursue other measures.

How many times have you received a personal thank you in the form of a phone call or hand-written card in the last year? For many of you it would take only one hand to tabulate the answer. Yes, the quick reply to an email which says thank you counts. The question you may ask yourself is, "Did the method and communication of the reply reflect the amount of time and effort the individual put into assisting you?"

The way a hand written thank you has impacted my career is too great to list. One specific example was the impact it had on moving my career into my real passion and love – training. A depth of my expertise was gained in my role as a trainer and coach in a company called Executive Speaking, Inc. It was my mentorship experience in presentation training for Senior Level Executives. I had brought a stamped, addressed, thank you to my interview. Upon completion of the interview I stopped in the lobby and wrote a personal note to the CEO thanking her for the opportunity and expressing my interest in the job. I dropped the card in the mailbox on my way out. After receiving the job from 200 considered applications I learned the personal thank you was an indication to the CEO of how I would treat her clients.

Bringing old fashioned manners into your interaction with clients may bring you the competitive edge.

Time is our most precious commodity in today's work environment. With cut backs and tight budgets increasing everyone's work load, the gift of time is the greatest gift a client will provide you.

A hand written thank you note takes moments yet it can indicate you will pay them specific and customized attention – you might even include this use of positive language in your note.

Before sending an Instant Message (IM) with your need, politely asking a person if they have a moment to answer a question shows respect for whatever task or meeting the person maybe involved in. I frequently ask the focus of the question and request the individual to give me a call rather than trying to comprehend the depth of the question or concern in the short phrases often used in IM.

A card expressing sorrow for a loss, a card celebrating a birth in the family or a card congratulating a colleague on completing a certification course can build a relationship in a quiet, respectful way. No, I do not own stock in a greeting card company, I simply have heard over and over again from team members and clients how the relationship patterns of the past have been forgotten and how much a personal touch makes a person feel like an appreciated colleague or client – you will be treating their life and their dreams with dignity.

Ensure your apologies are sincere or don't bother

We all have the need to build a bridge when an action did not have the intended results we hoped for or when we have an emotional moment and violate our desire to treat each other with dignity and respect.

Begin by thinking how the other person was impacted – not about your own embarrassment.

As you begin your phone call ask the individual if they have a moment. Don't add insult to injury by just blurting out your apology because you have finally worked up the courage to apologize. When it's the right time, let the individual know you would like to apologize and be specific. Let them know what you have learned from the experience and how you will temper your response in the future. The individual may or may actively acknowledge they accept you apology – in fact they maybe in a bit of shock as sincere apologies are far too few in the work place. Ask them if there is anything you can clear up for them and if there are no additional concerns, thank them for their time.

Team members often report that a half-hearted, or flip apology is worse than no apology at all. Take the time to think through the situation and be willing to apologize in humility and with the respect for the other person's perspective.

Where else do manners display dignity and respect?

When someone shares something they will believe will be helpful and you were already aware of the information, reply with respect. A simply thank you for the information is polite – "I already knew that" or "Yes, I am very aware of that" is not. There is no faster way to shut down a colleague or client than with an attitude of arrogance.

When someone asks a question, treat each question with dignity and respect.

The following words are harsh and lack old-fashioned manners by reprimanding the person who asked the question:

- Obviously – If it was obvious to the individual he/she would not have asked the question
- As I said – This implies the person was not paying attention when no individual can process all that is being said in a lengthy meeting
- Let me make this clear – This implication implies someone did not understand and if they didn't understand perhaps it was the way you presented the information
- That has nothing to do with this conversation – Clearly the individual believes it does and you can simply be curious and ask, "Help me understand how this information matches this situation?"
- You should have – Perhaps the individual didn't know how, didn't have the authority to do the task or wasn't aware it was even an option – talk about how you can proceed in the future

When someone thanks you for your help, eliminate the phrase "no problem" from your vocabulary. Why would someone bother to thank you again if you quickly dismiss the time and energy it took for them to appreciate your help?

Old fashioned manners include the art of graciousness. You are welcome is the response to thank you. My pleasure to assist you is another response. To respond to a client with the phrase no problem implies it might have even crossed your mind the client request was a problem for you! This casual phrase has become a response of client service specialists and retail workers nation-wide and it is exhausting.

Treating those within your sphere of influence with the twist of old-fashioned manners is upholding your privilege and responsibility of your client facing role or your leadership role.

Twist Five: Make a Big Deal of Success

One of the saddest laments of team member today is how few celebrations there are for the accomplishment of goals. They report the meetings go something like this:

- The project was accepted by management, thanks.
- What we need to do now is... and it has to be done by...

Celebrations show dignity and respect for the team members who accomplished goals or for the client who has achieved a milestone. Do you notice your client's successes or simply focus on how they are helping your success?

What defines a "Big Deal"?

The specific acknowledgement of specific contributions to the success. Big deal does not necessarily imply a financial investment. The easy and simple summary of one key role each individual contributed to the completion of the project will be a big change and be seen as a big deal to many.

It may sound something like this:

- Thank you John for the way you helped keep us in check concerning our budget along the way.
- Vanessa, your contribution of overseeing our partner's contribution to the project was greatly appreciated.
- Kyle, without your eye for detail the proposal would not has been as accurate as it is and I know it will help us in winning the deal.
- Max, your willingness to push us for creative solutions contributed to defining our competitive edge in new ways and I thank you.

My guess is your team would be running to the conference lines for meetings if their specific contributions were acknowledged and appreciated.

Big Deals may involve some form of compensation. Remember your story of motivation may not be your teams' form of motivation. Don't make up their story – ask them. Some individuals are motivated by cash compensation, some are motivated by recognition amongst peer and superiors and some are motivated by incentive prizes.

Why the difference you ask? Individuals are at different phases in their life and may be seeking recognition to build their resume, some may prefer a prize they can cherish because cash is not an issue or would just go to a bill, and others only feel like it's a true incentive if they can choose what is important for them and cash is the choice.

If you have influence over large forms of recognition, please have the dignity and respect of surveying the potential winners as to what a "Big Deal" would be for them. The days of a company trip, even if spouses or significant others are included, have diminished. With two working parents and individuals living away from immediate relatives, trips may actually be more of a hindrance than an incentive. For positions which require travel as part of the routine of business – travel may be the last incentive a person would embrace.

Upon winning a Sales and Service award for a large financial institution I learned my "Big Deal" was a trip to Disney World and spouses/partners were included. I was single, traveled 75% if the time for business and had no interest in seeing Disney World again. My positive experience came from inviting my brother whom as a teacher would not be rewarded for his work with such a trip and it provided me an opportunity to advance my relationship with him who resided in another state.

Other ideas for "Big Deals"

- A simple card mailed or placed on the individual's desk with specific appreciation for specific contribution
- Distribution of positive comments about the team or individuals on the team from Senior Management
- Any form of acknowledgement provided by a client to the team which assisted them
- The success of a sale or retention of a client because of a solution by an internal team or team member

The dignity many leaders miss is the communication of how the role of the team contributes to the big picture goals of the company. It is so respectful to consistently and constantly share with individuals how their hard work is an important contribution.

The twist of "Big Deals" taps into the most basic of human needs – the need to feel the time and effort they put into their responsibilities matter.

5 Tiny Twists to bringing dignity and respect back to the workplace comes from the ideas and desires expressed by hundreds of salespeople, client service specialists, emerging leaders and even a few select leaders who have already "made it" and find company mission statements not being supported by daily communication patterns.

Fast Track to Significant Conversations: Content would provide you a thought process and repeatable, consistent system to prepare for meetings, conference calls and even spontaneous interactions because significant conversations happen at insignificant times, not just in formal presentations.

BethAnn uses the system in presentation seminars and private coaching with video-taped feedback to help people fast forward their careers and build patterns of communication with dignity and respect.

BethAnn would be happy to send you her Fast Track to Significant Conversations: Presence as gift – simply connect with her on her web page or email shown in the front of the book.

www.ingramcontent.com/pod-product-compliance
Lightning Source LLC
Chambersburg PA
CBHW070725180526
45167CB00004B/1620